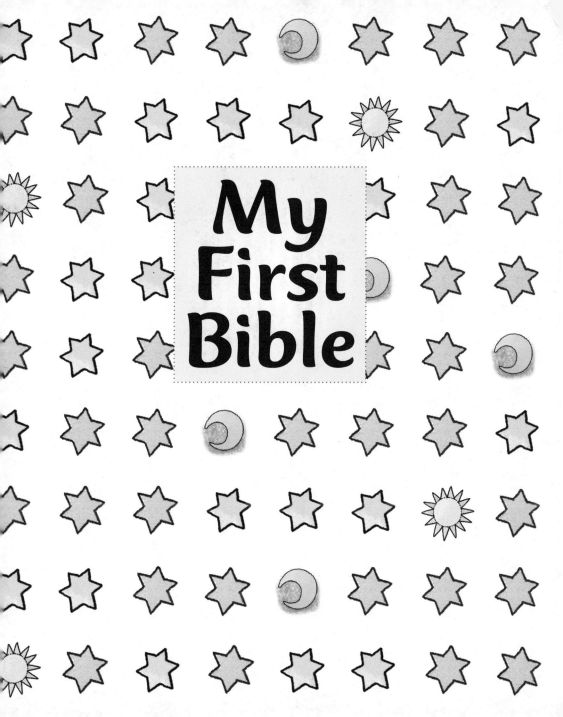

My
First
Bible

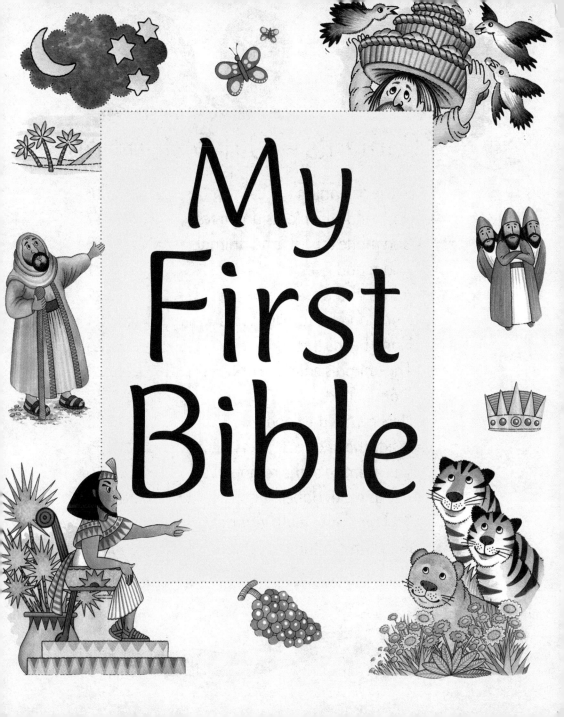

My First Bible

Contents — Old Testament

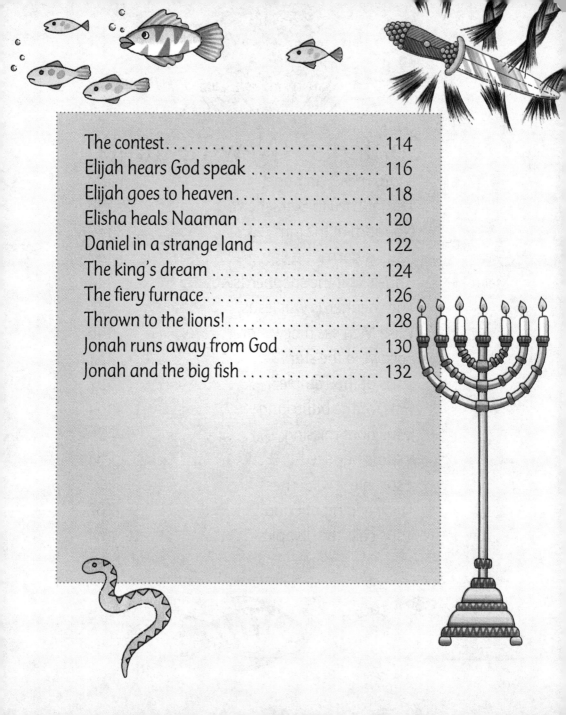

Contents — New Testament

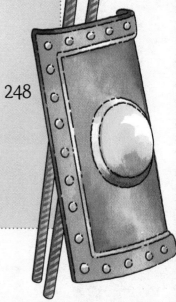

The Old
Testament

In the beginning

Genesis 1:1–10, 14–16

A very, very long time ago, at the beginning of time, God created the world out of nothing through His Word.

God made the light and the darkness.
God made huge, tall mountains.
God made deep blue seas and oceans.
God made the round earth to spin, the fiery sun to shine, and the silvery moon to glow. God made twinkling stars and mysterious planets.

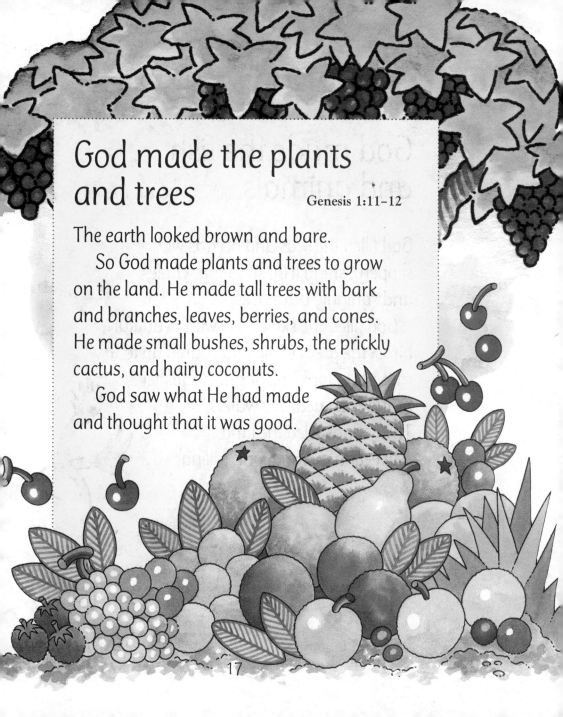

God made the plants and trees

Genesis 1:11–12

The earth looked brown and bare.

So God made plants and trees to grow on the land. He made tall trees with bark and branches, leaves, berries, and cones. He made small bushes, shrubs, the prickly cactus, and hairy coconuts.

God saw what He had made and thought that it was good.

17

God made the fish and animals

Genesis 1:20–25

God filled the seas and oceans with
slippery, shiny fish, spouting whales,
and squiggly octopuses.
    God filled the sky above with beautiful
birds: the great eagle that soared up to the
mountain tops, the bright kingfisher
that darted near the water.
Their songs filled the land:
    tweeting, cawing, and trilling.

God made animals of every kind:
tall and short, prickly and furry,
striped and spotted
and patterned.
They roamed freely
and ate the lush,
green grass
and plants.

Adam and Eve

Genesis 1:26–31; 2:8–15

"Now I will make people," said God.

God created Adam and Eve — a man and a woman. They could think and feel and love. God made them in His image, which means they were holy like Him. He asked them to look after the animals.

God made a beautiful place for them to live in called the Garden of Eden. God was pleased with everything He had made. It was very good.

21

Adam and Eve sin

Genesis 2:16–17; 3:1–24

God told Adam, "You may eat the fruit from any tree in the garden except from the tree of knowledge of good and evil. If you eat that tree's fruit, you will die."

But the serpent said to Eve, "You won't really die, you know. Have a taste. It's good!"

So Eve took the fruit and had a bite. Then she gave some to Adam. He ate some too. Adam and Eve had broken God's rules. God was very angry because they sinned and sent them out of the garden of Eden forever. God punished Adam and Eve for disobeying, but He promised to send His people a Savior to take away their sin.

Noah and his family

Genesis 6:9–12, 17

Faithful Noah was a good man. He listened and believed when God spoke to him.

Noah had a wife and three sons: Shem, Ham, and Japheth.

Sadly, the world was no longer the good place God had made.

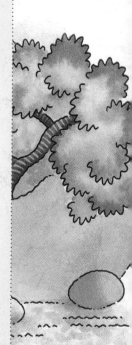

Sin brought trouble to the world. People were fighting each other. God was angry. He told Noah what He planned to do. God was going to send a great flood to cover the whole earth because of sin.

Noah builds the ark

Genesis 6:14–16

God told Noah to build a huge wooden boat called an ark:

"Get some good strong wood to build the boat, and cover it inside and out with tar. Put a roof on the top and build rooms inside. Put a door on one side. When the flood comes, you will be safe."

Noah did as God said. People watched and wondered. They even laughed at him! Why was he building a boat so far from the sea?

The animals enter the ark

Genesis 7:1–5

God wanted there to be animals on the earth after the flood.

So God told Noah to bring animals, birds, and reptiles into the ark, male and female of every kind.

"I will send rain for forty days and nights," said God, "and a great flood will cover every living thing in the world."

Only Noah, his family, and the animals would be safe inside the ark.

Storing food

Genesis 6:21–22

God told Noah to store up enough food to feed all the animals in the ark and enough for his own family too. That was a lot of food!

Noah and his sons worked hard to get everything ready.

They collected food from the land and stored it in the ark. When the flood came, there would be no more food to eat until it all grew again, fresh and new.

Here comes the flood!

Genesis 7:11–24

When the ark was ready, Noah and his family went inside. God closed the door.

Water burst up from the ground. Then the rain began to pour down. It rained and it rained, for forty days and nights.

First the water covered the land. Then it covered the trees. Soon even the tallest mountains were hidden by water!

Nothing was left alive on the earth except for Noah and his family and the animals in the ark. God kept them very safe.

Inside the ark

Genesis 7:23–24

Inside the ark, they were warm and safe. Noah and his family heard the rain drumming on the roof.

They saw the water all around the ark.

The animals were noisy, especially when it came to feeding time. But there was enough food for everyone.

All they could do now was wait for the rain to stop.

The promise of the rainbow

Genesis 8:4, 15–19; 9:8–17

At long last, the rain stopped. God sent wind to dry the water. Dry land appeared!

The ark came to rest on the mountains of Ararat.

Noah came out of the ark. He praised God for saving his family and keeping them alive.

God put a beautiful rainbow in the sky as a promise that He would never send another flood to cover the whole earth. When we see a rainbow, we can remember that God keeps His promises, especially His promise to save us from our sin through His Son, Jesus.

37

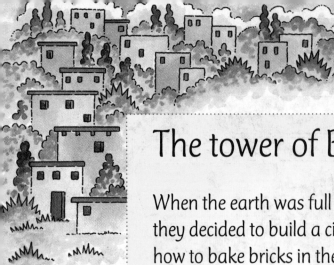

The tower of Babel

Genesis 11:1–9

When the earth was full of people again, they decided to build a city. They learned how to bake bricks in the sun and stuck them together with tar.

"Let's build a tower that reaches to the sky!" they said. "Everyone will see how important we are."

But God saw what they were planning. He knew they were forgetting about Him.

So God mixed up their languages. They couldn't understand each other anymore! It all sounded like babble.

God scattered the people all over the earth and they stopped building the city.

God's promise to Abraham

Genesis 12:1-2

Abraham was a good man.

God promised that Abraham's children would bless the earth. The problem was, Abraham and his wife Sarah could not have any children.

"Abraham!" said God. "Look at the stars and try to count them. You will have as many people in your family as the number of stars you can see."

Abraham believed God's special promise. He was willing to wait.

Sure enough, when Abraham was ninety-nine years old, God's promise came true. Abraham and Sarah had a baby boy.

Abraham and Sarah were so happy that they named their son "Isaac," which means "laughter." Abraham and Isaac were Jesus' ancestors.

Rebekah's kindness

Genesis 24:1–61

Rebekah was a beautiful girl. She was also very kind. Every day she fetched water from the well for her family.

One afternoon, she noticed a man standing at the well with his ten camels.

Rebekah offered a drink of water to the man and his camels. God had told the man that this would be a sign that this was the girl to be Isaac's wife.

Then the man took a beautiful gold ring and gold bracelets out of his bag and put them on Rebekah. She had never seen anything so fine!

"Take me to your father's house," he said.

So they set off to see Rebekah's family. The man said that he had come to find a wife for Abraham's son, Isaac. He asked if Rebekah would be Isaac's wife. She agreed and set off the next day to marry Isaac.

43

Isaac and Rebekah have twins

Genesis 25:19–28

Isaac and Rebekah were very happy together.

After a few years, they had twin boys called Esau and Jacob.

Although they were twins, the boys were very different.

Esau had red hair and he was hairy all over. He loved hunting and being outdoors with his bow and arrows.

Jacob had smooth skin. He loved being at home.

44

He was a good cook and made wonderful soups and stews for his family.

Esau was born first. This meant that when Isaac, their father, died, Esau would be given all that his father owned and a special blessing.

Jacob secretly wanted to be the one to get the blessing and all that his father had, so he planned a nasty trick.

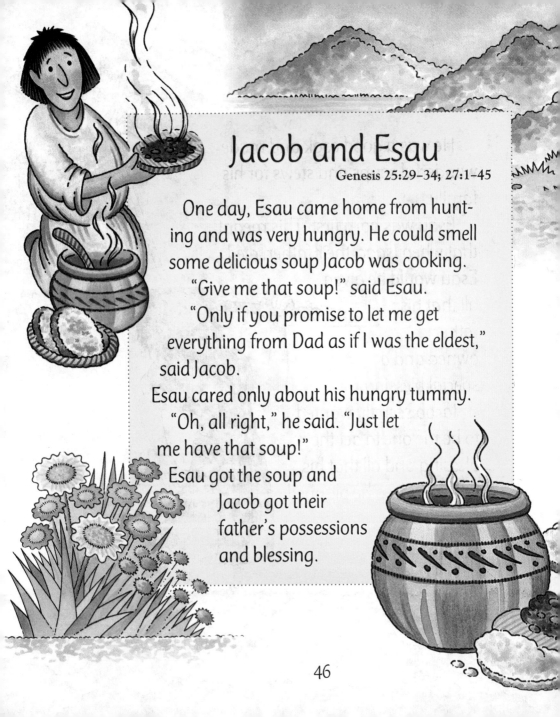

Jacob and Esau

Genesis 25:29–34; 27:1–45

One day, Esau came home from hunting and was very hungry. He could smell some delicious soup Jacob was cooking.

"Give me that soup!" said Esau.

"Only if you promise to let me get everything from Dad as if I was the eldest," said Jacob.

Esau cared only about his hungry tummy.

"Oh, all right," he said. "Just let me have that soup!"

Esau got the soup and Jacob got their father's possessions and blessing.

A few years later, Jacob tricked their father, too, when he was dying.

He dressed up in goat's skin so his skin would feel hairy, like his brother's. Their old father could not see well and thought it was Esau. So he gave Jacob the special blessing. Esau was furious when he found out.

Jacob ran away from home. It was years later that he came back and said he was sorry to Esau for the nasty tricks he had played.

Joseph and his brothers

Genesis 35:23–26

Abraham believed that God would keep His promise and give him a big family.

And God kept His promise.

Abraham's grandson, Jacob, had a very large family. He had twelve sons and a daughter. He lived with his family in the land of Canaan.

Jacob's sons looked after his sheep and goats.

Jacob's sons were called Reuben, Simeon, Levi, Judah, Issachar, Zebulun, Dan, Naphtali, Gad, Asher, Joseph, and Benjamin.

Of all his sons, Jacob loved Joseph the most. Joseph was Jacob's favorite son.

Joseph's new coat

Genesis 37:3–4

When Joseph was seventeen years old, his father, Jacob, gave him a very special present. He gave him a wonderful new coat to wear.

Joseph was very proud of his new coat. He strutted around in front of all his brothers, saying, "Look at me! Look what Dad has bought for me!"

But Joseph's brothers were jealous.

"Why does Dad love Joseph more than us?" they muttered.

"Why haven't we been given coats like that?" they grumbled.

Joseph didn't seem to hear them. He thought only about his coat.

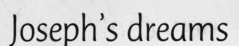

Joseph's dreams

Genesis 37:5–11

One night, Joseph had a very strange dream. He dreamed there were eleven sheaves of grain, that all bowed down to his sheaf.

Then he dreamed he saw eleven stars, the sun and the moon, all bowing down to him!

Joseph told his family all about his dreams. But it made his brothers very angry.

"Why does Joseph think he is more important than us?" they asked.

"Do you think you are going to be a king and rule over us, Joseph?" they mocked.

Joseph's brothers were very jealous.

Joseph is sold as a slave

Genesis 37:12–35

One day when all the brothers were in the fields looking after the sheep, they thought up a cruel plan to get rid of Joseph. They had heard enough of his stories about grain and stars bowing to him!

When Joseph came to see them, they threw him into an empty well. They were planning to leave him there to die, but then a group of travelling traders came past. They were on their way to Egypt. The brothers quickly changed their plan and sold Joseph to the traders.

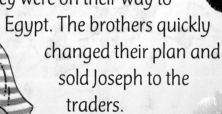

54

He was taken away as a slave!

The brothers told their father that Joseph had been killed by a wild animal. They thought they would never see Joseph again.

But God had other plans for Joseph.

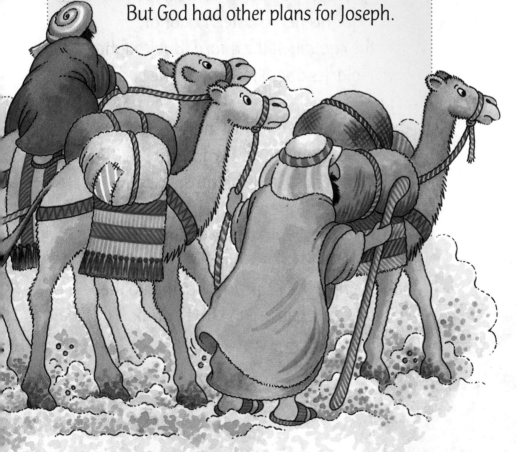

Joseph
understands dreams

Genesis 39:1–40:23

Joseph worked hard in Egypt
for his new master, Potiphar,
the captain of the guard. But Potiphar's
wife told lies about Joseph and he ended up
in jail!

In jail, Joseph met the king's chief baker
and the king's wine steward. One night they
both had very strange dreams. Joseph
understood the dreams.

The wine steward spoke first: "I saw a
grapevine with three branches. The grapes
became ripe and I squeezed them into the
king's cup and gave it to him to drink."

Joseph told him happily that in three days he would be freed from jail.

The baker spoke next, but his dream did not end so happily.

"I was carrying three baskets of cakes and pastries, when some birds swooped down and ate them all up!" said the baker.

Joseph looked very sad, and said, "I'm sorry to say, you will never be free. The king means to kill you in three days!"

Three days later, the dreams came true, just as Joseph had said!

Joseph helps Pharaoh

Genesis 41:1–41

Two years later, the king of Egypt began to have strange dreams that no one could understand. The wine steward, whom Joseph had helped in jail, remembered Joseph and told the king all about him.

Joseph was brought before the great king of Egypt.

"Your majesty, tell me your dreams," said Joseph.

"I was standing on the river bank when seven fat cows came out of the river to feed," said the king. "Then seven thin cows came and ate them all up.

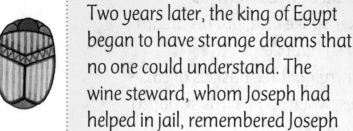

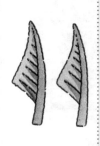

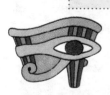

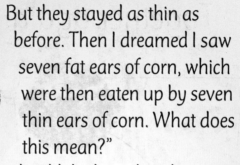

But they stayed as thin as before. Then I dreamed I saw seven fat ears of corn, which were then eaten up by seven thin ears of corn. What does this mean?"

Joseph told the king that there would be a time of great famine in the land. He must store up food for seven years to feed the people because there would be no food for the seven years after that.

The king was pleased with what Joseph said and put him in charge of storing food for Egypt.

Together again

Genesis 42:1–8; 45; 46:1–7

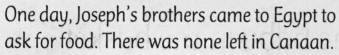

One day, Joseph's brothers came to Egypt to ask for food. There was none left in Canaan.

They did not recognize their brother Joseph. Many years had passed and Joseph was older now.

They begged for food to take home to their father in Canaan.

When Joseph told them who he really was, they cried and said they were sorry for what they had done to him all those years before.

Once again, the family was back together. Joseph's father, Jacob, came to Egypt to live until the end of his days.

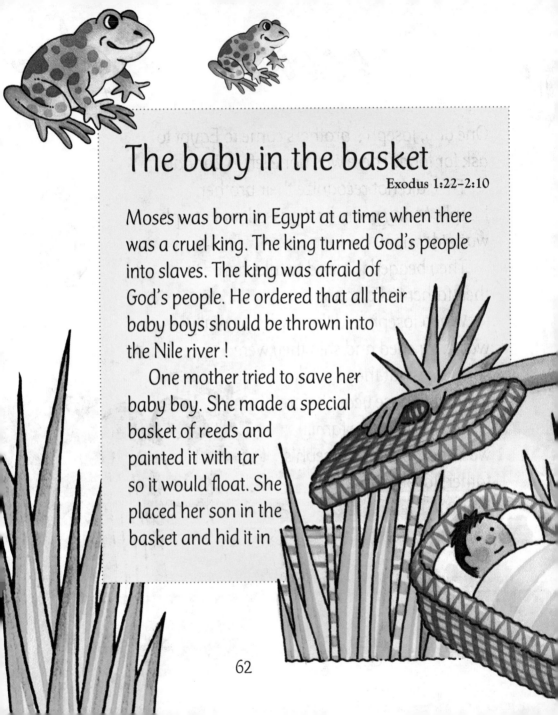

The baby in the basket

Exodus 1:22–2:10

Moses was born in Egypt at a time when there was a cruel king. The king turned God's people into slaves. The king was afraid of God's people. He ordered that all their baby boys should be thrown into the Nile river !

One mother tried to save her baby boy. She made a special basket of reeds and painted it with tar so it would float. She placed her son in the basket and hid it in

the long bulrushes at the side of the river. The baby's sister, Miriam, hid close by and watched.

A royal princess came to the river to bathe and heard the baby crying. She lifted him out of the basket. She wanted to help the baby.

Miriam stepped out from behind the bulrushes.

"I know who can feed the baby!" she said to the princess.

She fetched her mother. So Moses was looked after by his own mother.

When he was old enough, he went to live in the palace with the princess.

Moses runs away

Exodus 2:11–15

When Moses grew up, he saw how cruelly his people were treated by the king.

Once he saw an Egyptian beating a slave. Moses was furious. He looked to see if anyone was watching, then he stepped forward and killed the Egyptian.

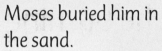

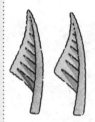

Moses buried him in the sand.

The next day, Moses saw two slaves fighting and tried to stop them.

One of them said, "Well, are you going to kill me next, like you killed that Egyptian yesterday?"

Moses was very afraid: someone had seen him after all.

Moses ran away, far from the king's palace, to a land called Midian.

The burning bush

Exodus 3:1–10

Moses became a shepherd. One day, he saw a very strange sight: a bush on fire. Flames crackled and licked the dry branches, but the bush did not burn up! In fact, it was the angel of the Lord!

A voice from inside the bush called: "Moses! Moses!"

Moses trembled and stepped closer to the bush. Could it be God speaking?

"Take off your sandals," said God. "You are standing on holy ground."

Moses covered his eyes.

"I am the God of your father, the God of Abraham, the God of Isaac,

and the
God of
Jacob,"
said God.
"I have heard
My people's cries
for help. I want you
to go to the cruel king
and bring My people
out of Egypt. I will give
them a new land of
their own, which
will be full of
good things."

The plagues of Egypt

Exodus 7:14–11:8

Moses went to the king, but he would not let the people leave Egypt. So God sent terrible plagues to change the king's mind.

The water of the River Nile turned to blood.

Then hundreds of croak-ing frogs hopped into everyone's houses and beds! Next came gnats and flies,

68

which buzzed into the Egyptians' houses.

All the cows and sheep died. Then all the Egyptians were covered in boils and their skin became terribly sore. Still the king wouldn't change his mind.

Hailstones hit the land. Locusts came and devoured the crops. Darkness fell upon the land and no one could see.

But the last plague would be the most terrible of all. Moses warned the king that all the firstborn children of Egypt would die in one night.

69

The Passover feast

Exodus 12:1–8, 29–32

Moses told God's people to get ready.

"Take a lamb, kill it, and put some of the lamb's blood on the doorposts of the house," he said. "Roast the lamb over a fire and eat the meat with bitter herbs and bread made without yeast. This is the Passover."

That night, death came to Egypt. All the firstborn sons and animals of the Egyptians died. Even the king's son died.

But death passed over all the homes of God's people, and God saved them all.

The king said to Moses, "Go! Leave Egypt! Take your animals and go as you asked."

The king finally decided to let the people go.

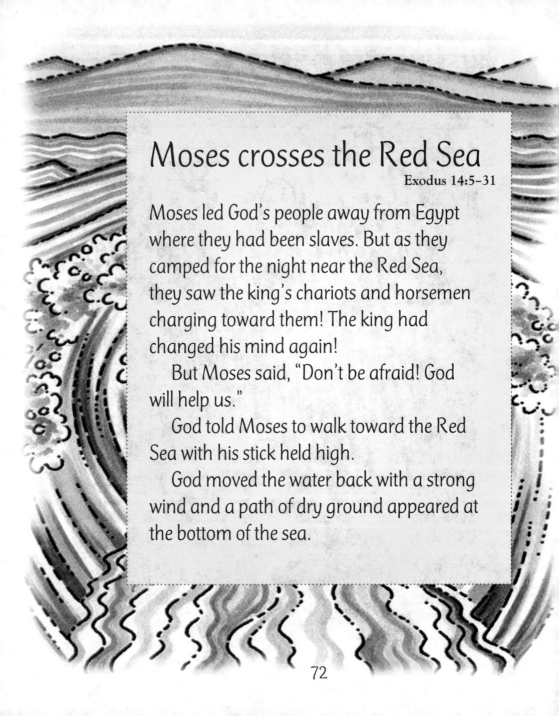

Moses crosses the Red Sea

Exodus 14:5–31

Moses led God's people away from Egypt where they had been slaves. But as they camped for the night near the Red Sea, they saw the king's chariots and horsemen charging toward them! The king had changed his mind again!

But Moses said, "Don't be afraid! God will help us."

God told Moses to walk toward the Red Sea with his stick held high.

God moved the water back with a strong wind and a path of dry ground appeared at the bottom of the sea.

Moses led his people across the path to safety on the other side of the Red Sea.

The Egyptian army tried to follow but their chariot wheels got stuck in the ground. Once again, God told Moses to hold out his hand over the water. The Red Sea came crashing back down over the Egyptian army.

Moses led his people on toward the new land God had promised to his people.

Food in the desert

Exodus 16:1–18

"We're hungry!" grumbled the people.

God had guided them across the Red Sea to safety on the other side, away from the Egyptian army and the cruel king at last. But now the Israelites were grumbling. And their stomachs were rumbling.

"I will send bread from heaven," said God to Moses. That evening, quail flew over the camp and the people caught them.

In the morning, dew covered the ground. When it had gone, there were flakes of white manna on the ground. It was the bread from heaven that God had sent. It tasted like wafers made with honey.

God had provided all they needed. He sent enough food for them each day.

God gives the Ten Commandments

Deuteronomy 5:1–22

Moses climbed Mount Sinai to talk to God. "I am the Lord your God, who rescued you when you were slaves in Egypt," said God. "Obey Me and I will make your nation great," said God.

"Do not pray to or praise any other gods but Me.

"Don't pray to statues, pictures, or things of the earth, sky or sea instead of Me.

"Think about how you use My name; do not swear or use My name carelessly.

"Remember the day of rest I give you at the end of the week.

"Love your mother and father and listen to what they say.

"Do not plot to kill anyone.

"Be faithful to your husband or wife.

"Do not steal.

"Do not tell lies about other people.

"Don't look greedily at things that belong to other people."

There was a trumpet blast and the words were written on stone tablets. These laws are called the Ten Commandments.

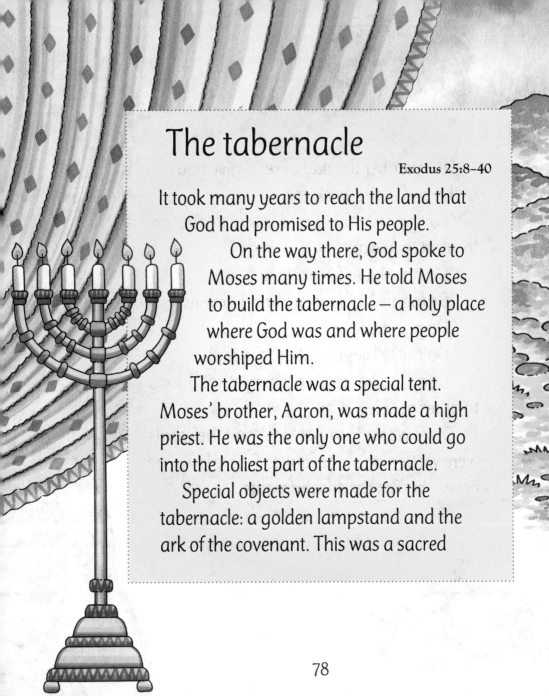

The tabernacle

Exodus 25:8–40

It took many years to reach the land that God had promised to His people.

On the way there, God spoke to Moses many times. He told Moses to build the tabernacle – a holy place where God was and where people worshiped Him.

The tabernacle was a special tent. Moses' brother, Aaron, was made a high priest. He was the only one who could go into the holiest part of the tabernacle.

Special objects were made for the tabernacle: a golden lampstand and the ark of the covenant. This was a sacred box that contained the stone tablets with the commandments God gave to Moses on Mount Sinai.

God's tabernacle was a very holy place. People came to say sorry to God for the wrong things they had done and to ask for God's blessing.

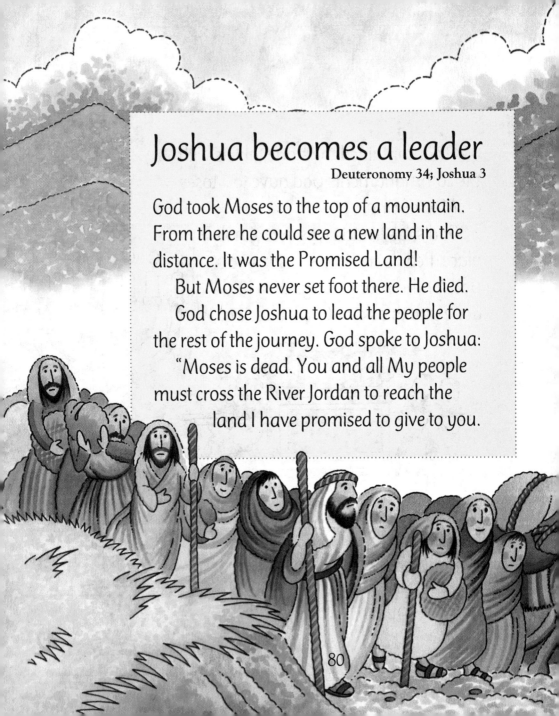

Joshua becomes a leader

Deuteronomy 34; Joshua 3

God took Moses to the top of a mountain. From there he could see a new land in the distance. It was the Promised Land!

But Moses never set foot there. He died. God chose Joshua to lead the people for the rest of the journey. God spoke to Joshua: "Moses is dead. You and all My people must cross the River Jordan to reach the land I have promised to give to you.

I will be with you, as I always was with Moses. I will never leave you. Be brave."

Joshua ordered the officers of the people to be prepared to cross the river.

The priests went on ahead, carrying the ark of the covenant from the tabernacle. The water stopped flowing and the people crossed the river on dry ground. It was a miracle.

Joshua and the walls of Jericho

Joshua 6:1–21

To reach the Promised Land, God's people had to get past the city of Jericho.

The city had huge, thick stone walls. It seemed impossible to get through. But God had a plan.

God told Joshua to choose seven priests with trumpets made of rams' horns. He said they must march around the city once every day for six days, blowing their trumpets, following the ark of the covenant.

On the seventh day, the priests had to march round six times. Then on the seventh time, the priests sounded a long trumpet blast on their horns, the people shouted and...the mighty walls of Jericho fell to the ground.

God had given them the city of Jericho.

84

Gideon's victory

Judges 6:11–7:22

Years later, when Joshua died, God's people began to turn away from God and His Commandments. So God sent judges to guide the people. One of the judges was Gideon.

Gideon was chosen to lead the army. He knew that God was on his side and would help him. They had to fight the strong Midianite army.

Gideon gave each soldier a ram's horn trumpet and a jar with a burning torch inside.

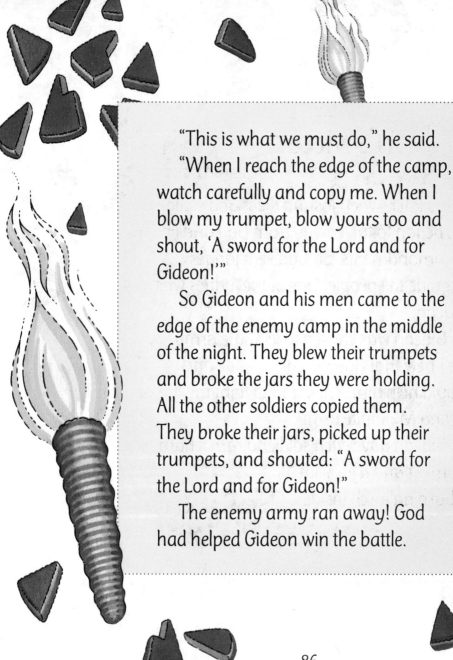

"This is what we must do," he said. "When I reach the edge of the camp, watch carefully and copy me. When I blow my trumpet, blow yours too and shout, 'A sword for the Lord and for Gideon!'"

So Gideon and his men came to the edge of the enemy camp in the middle of the night. They blew their trumpets and broke the jars they were holding. All the other soldiers copied them. They broke their jars, picked up their trumpets, and shouted: "A sword for the Lord and for Gideon!"

The enemy army ran away! God had helped Gideon win the battle.

The strength of Samson

Judges 14:5–6; 16:4–30

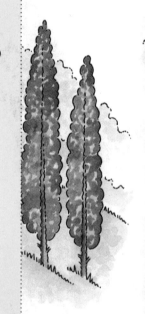

God had made Samson a very strong man. He could kill a lion with his bare hands. Samson had long hair, that was braided in seven braids. If his hair was ever cut, his strength would go. But that was a secret.

The Philistines were enemies of God's people. They wanted to find out the secret of Samson's strength so they could defeat him. They paid a woman named Delilah to find out the secret.

Delilah asked Samson many times. Finally he told her about his hair.

Delilah told the Philistines,
and when Samson was asleep,
the Philistines cut off his hair! They captured
Samson and threw him into prison.

But Samson's hair started to grow again.

Samson was kept in chains. One day, when
the Philistines were meeting in their temple,
Samson pushed against the pillars of the
temple with all his might.

God gave Samson strength one more time.

The temple fell down with a mighty crash
and all the Philistines were crushed beneath
the great pillars.

Ruth

Ruth 1–4

Naomi was sad. She had left her home to find food in another land because there was none in Israel. Then her husband and her sons had died. Naomi was all alone except for Ruth and Orpah, the wives of her sons.

Naomi got ready to travel home. Ruth was very kind and would not leave Naomi.

"Where you go, I will go," said Ruth. "Your people will be my people, and your God will be my God."

Ruth worked hard all day, gathering leftover corn from the edges of the harvest fields. She made bread to feed Naomi and herself.

The farmer of the fields, Boaz, watched Ruth and saw how good and kind she was to Naomi. Before long, Boaz asked Ruth to marry him! They had a baby boy called Obed.

Naomi held her grandson, Obed, lovingly in her arms. She had once been so sad, but now God had given her great happiness.

Samuel
listens to God

1 Samuel 3:1–18

Samuel was a young boy who lived in the Temple. He helped Eli, the priest, look after the lampstand.

One night, after Samuel had gone to bed, he heard a voice calling his name: "Samuel! Samuel!"

Samuel ran to Eli. "Here I am. You called me," he said.

But Eli told him to go back to bed. "I didn't call you!"

Then Samuel heard the voice again.

He ran straight to Eli.

"Here I am!" he said.

"No, I did not call you!" said Eli.

It happened a third time.

Then Eli realized that it must be God calling and said to Samuel, "Next time you hear Him calling, say, 'Here I am, Lord, your servant is listening.'"

Samuel went back to bed and he heard God's voice again.

Samuel did as Eli said and listened carefully to God. God told him many things. In the morning Samuel told Eli all about it.

Samuel was only a young boy, but God had chosen him to be a special messenger.

David the shepherd boy

1 Samuel 16:11–13

David was a shepherd boy. He looked after his father's sheep on the hills. He led them to pastures of green grass. He took them to streams of clear water where they could drink.

If one of the sheep was lost, David would look everywhere for it until he found it.

Sometimes there was danger. Wild animals tried to snatch the sheep and lambs. If a lion or a bear tried to carry off one of the flock, David would kill it. He was very brave.

David played the harp and sang songs to God.

God had a plan for David. He told Samuel to anoint David to be the next king of Israel.

David plays for King Saul

1 Samuel 16:14–23

King Saul became a very troubled man because he had not done what God had told him to do. He often sat in his room feeling terrible. His servants thought it might help him to listen to some music.

"There is a boy in Bethlehem," said one servant, "who is very good at playing the harp. His name is David. He takes care of his father's sheep."

Saul asked them to fetch David.
Saul did not know that David had been
anointed by Samuel to be the next king.

King Saul listened to David playing
the harp and the music helped
him to feel calm again.

"Stay here," he said to
David. "I wish to hear more."

So David stayed with
the king. Whenever
the king felt terrible,
David would play
beautiful music
on his harp.

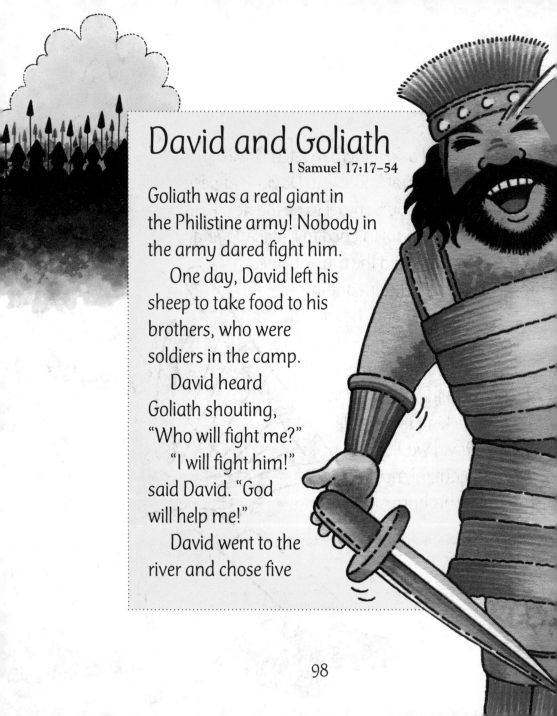

David and Goliath
1 Samuel 17:17–54

Goliath was a real giant in the Philistine army! Nobody in the army dared fight him.

One day, David left his sheep to take food to his brothers, who were soldiers in the camp.

David heard Goliath shouting, "Who will fight me?"

"I will fight him!" said David. "God will help me!"

David went to the river and chose five

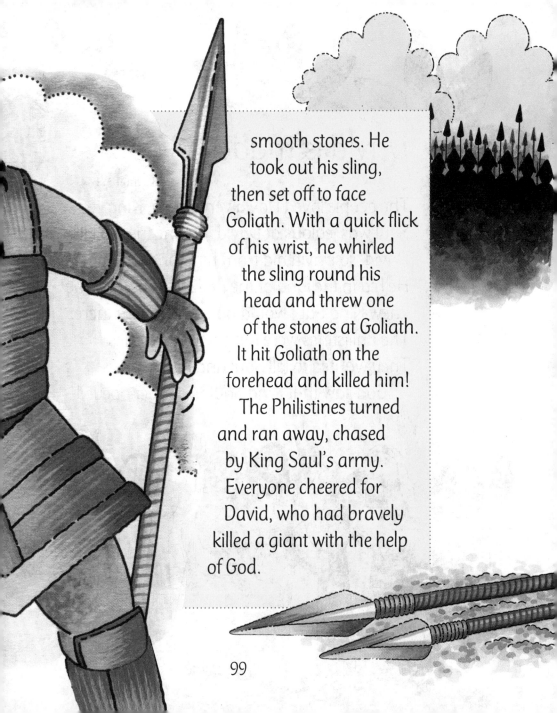

smooth stones. He took out his sling, then set off to face Goliath. With a quick flick of his wrist, he whirled the sling round his head and threw one of the stones at Goliath. It hit Goliath on the forehead and killed him! The Philistines turned and ran away, chased by King Saul's army. Everyone cheered for David, who had bravely killed a giant with the help of God.

David is made king

2 Samuel 5:1–4

The people loved David very much. King Saul was jealous of David, and he tried to kill David, so David hid from him for a long time. He hid in the land of the Philistines because he knew King Saul would not look for him there. The Philistines were King Saul's enemies. They wanted to kill Saul and his sons.

God saw that King Saul no longer obeyed

Him or ruled in a way that honored God.

The Philistines came after King Saul, and Saul and his sons were killed.

David was very sad when he heard the news. He had been good friends with Jonathan, Saul's son. David wept.

But many years before, Samuel had anointed David and now it was time for him to be king.

David was a strong ruler of God's people. He fought bravely against their enemies and people cheered as he rode by on his mighty horse.

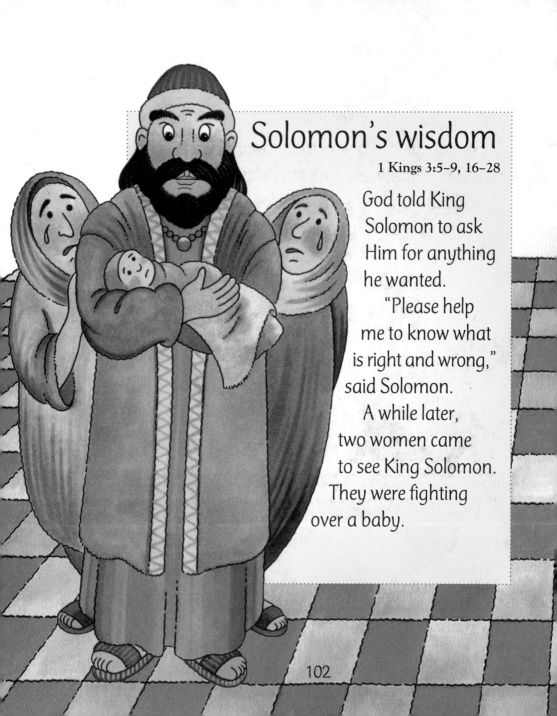

Solomon's wisdom

1 Kings 3:5–9, 16–28

God told King Solomon to ask Him for anything he wanted.

"Please help me to know what is right and wrong," said Solomon.

A while later, two women came to see King Solomon. They were fighting over a baby.

Each woman said she was the baby's mother. Solomon thought of a way to find out the truth.

"Fetch a sword," he said, "and cut the baby in half."

"Yes," said one woman. "Then at least we'll both get something."

"No!" shouted the other. "You mustn't hurt the baby. The other woman can keep him."

King Solomon knew at once that the real mother didn't want her baby to be hurt. Solomon gave her back the baby.

God had helped Solomon to decide wisely.

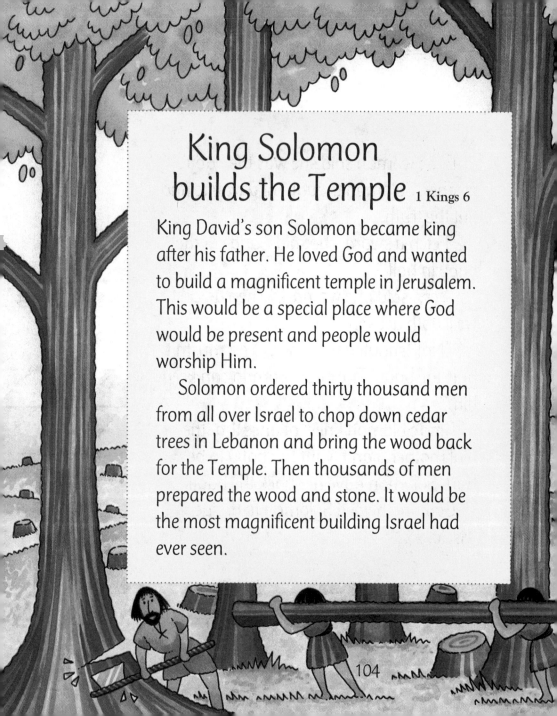

King Solomon builds the Temple 1 Kings 6

King David's son Solomon became king after his father. He loved God and wanted to build a magnificent temple in Jerusalem. This would be a special place where God would be present and people would worship Him.

Solomon ordered thirty thousand men from all over Israel to chop down cedar trees in Lebanon and bring the wood back for the Temple. Then thousands of men prepared the wood and stone. It would be the most magnificent building Israel had ever seen.

The inside of the Temple was lined with panels of cedar wood. Within the Temple Solomon prepared the Most Holy Place. The ark of the covenant would be kept there. Solomon had the inside of the Most Holy Place and the inside of the Temple covered with pure gold. He had huge angels made of olive wood to guard the inner room.

It took Solomon seven years to build the Temple. There had never been a finer building in Jerusalem.

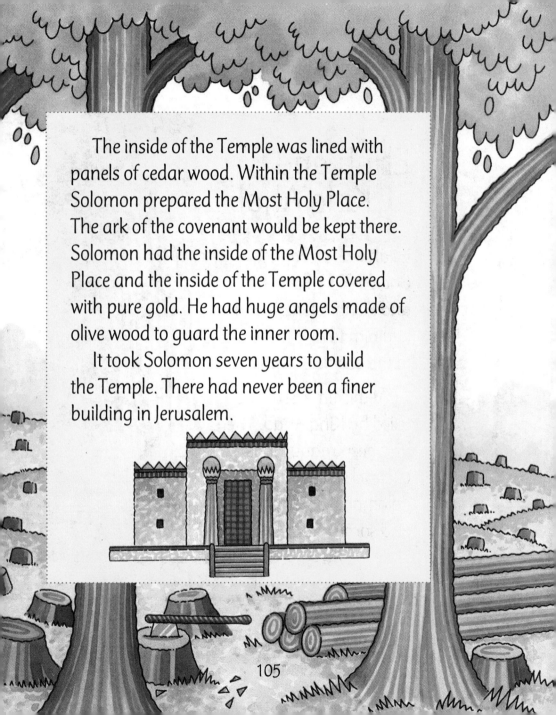

Elijah and King Ahab

1 Kings 17:1

Elijah was a prophet. God often spoke to him and Elijah listened. God told him to give messages to the people of Israel.

At this time Israel was ruled by King Ahab. There had been many kings of Israel since King Solomon, some good and some bad.

Ahab was one of the bad kings.

God gave Elijah a message for the king. Elijah knew he must go to King Ahab and speak firmly.

"Ahab!" said Elijah. "There is going to be a terrible drought. There will be no rain for many years. It will come only when God gives the word."

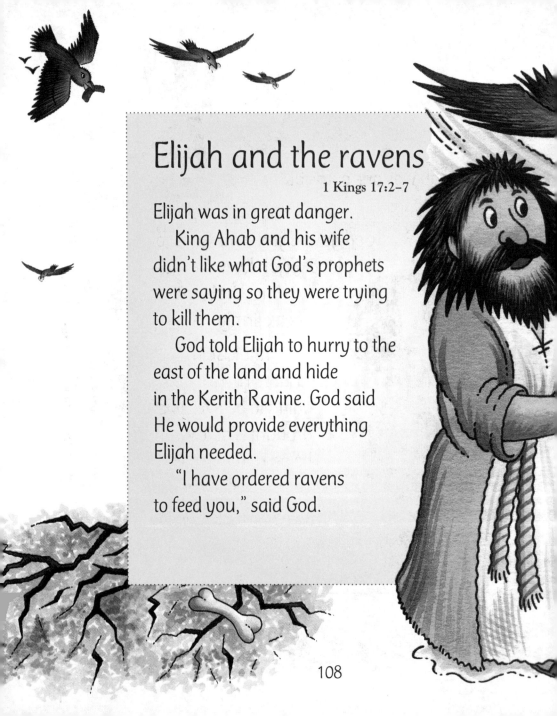

Elijah and the ravens

1 Kings 17:2–7

Elijah was in great danger.

King Ahab and his wife didn't like what God's prophets were saying so they were trying to kill them.

God told Elijah to hurry to the east of the land and hide in the Kerith Ravine. God said He would provide everything Elijah needed.

"I have ordered ravens to feed you," said God.

Sure enough, ravens brought Elijah bread and meat every morning and evening. Elijah drank the cool water from the brook in the ravine until it dried up.

God helped Elijah to stay alive and well.

Elijah and the widow

1 Kings 17:8–16

When the water in the brook ran dry, God told Elijah to go to Zarephath, where a widow would help him.

The widow had very little food. She lived with her young son. Both were very hungry. But she offered Elijah all she had left — a handful of flour in a jar and a little oil.

Elijah told the widow to go and make a small loaf of bread.

"Make some bread for me first, then for yourselves. God has told me that the jar of flour will never be empty and the jug of oil will never run dry, until

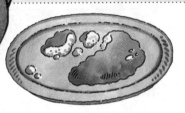

the day the rains come again!" said Elijah.
This is exactly what happened. So the
Lord provided again for all Elijah's needs.

Elijah and the prophets of Baal

1 Kings 18:20–24

After three years, God told Elijah to return to King Ahab.

Elijah spoke boldly to Ahab: "You have turned away from God and worshiped other gods like Baal instead."

Elijah knew that only his God, the God of Israel, was real and able to answer prayer.

"We will have a contest on Mount Carmel to see who is the true God," he said. "Get two bulls. The prophets of Baal can have one and put it on their altar. I will put the other on the altar of the Lord. Then the prophets of Baal can call upon him to send fire to burn up their offering. I will call on God to do the same. Whoever answers with fire is the true God."

The contest

1 Kings 18:25–39

The prophets of Baal called to Baal from morning till noon, but there was no fire.

"Shout louder!" said Elijah. "Perhaps Baal is asleep!"

Then Elijah prepared the altar of the Lord. He put the bull on it and soaked the altar with water. How could it possibly burn now?

Elijah prayed: "Oh, Lord God,

please show these people that You are the real God. Help them to know You and worship You again." Suddenly God sent fire to burn up the bull on the altar and all the water around it. Everyone was amazed! They threw themselves to the ground, shouting, "The Lord is God!" God had sent fire and shown King Ahab that He was the true God.

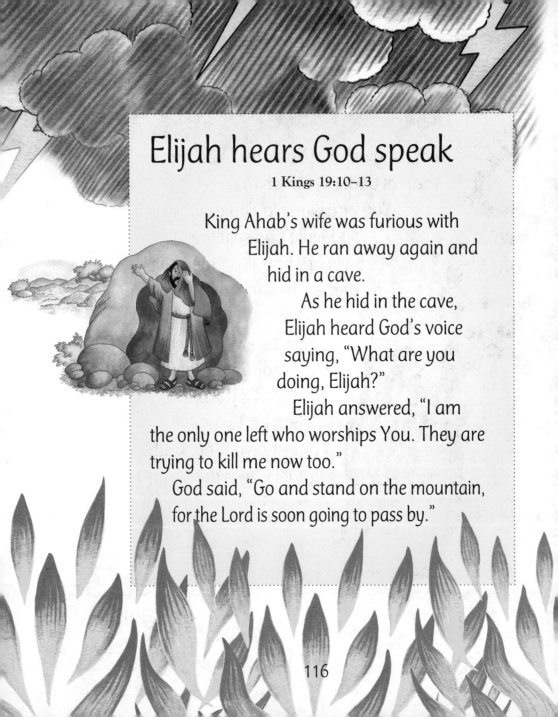

Elijah hears God speak

1 Kings 19:10–13

King Ahab's wife was furious with Elijah. He ran away again and hid in a cave.

As he hid in the cave, Elijah heard God's voice saying, "What are you doing, Elijah?"

Elijah answered, "I am the only one left who worships You. They are trying to kill me now too."

God said, "Go and stand on the mountain, for the Lord is soon going to pass by."

A mighty wind blew against the mountain so hard that rocks shattered. But God was not in the wind.

There was a mighty earthquake. But God was not in the earthquake.

There was a great fire. But God was not in the fire.

Then there was a gentle whisper. When Elijah heard it, he hid his face in his cloak and stood at the mouth of the cave. God was in the gentle whisper. He assured Elijah that he was not alone, but that other believers still worshiped God too.

Elijah goes to heaven

1 Kings 19:19–21; 2 Kings 2:11–12

Elijah chose Elisha to be the next prophet. Elisha became his close friend and helper.

At the end of Elijah's life, Elijah and Elisha were travelling along a road from Gilgal.

"I will not leave you," said Elisha to Elijah.

Suddenly a chariot of fire and horses of fire appeared. Then Elijah went up to heaven in a whirlwind.

Elisha watched and cried out, "My father! My father! The chariots and horsemen of Israel!" Elijah was gone from his sight.

119

Elisha heals Naaman

2 Kings 5

Naaman was an army general in another country.

Naaman had a skin disease called leprosy, which made his skin turn very white and sore. None of the doctors could help him.

He and his wife looked after a little girl from Israel. The little girl told Naaman about Elisha.

"God uses him to make people well again!" she said to Naaman.

So Naaman set out to see Elisha. But Elisha would not see Naaman.

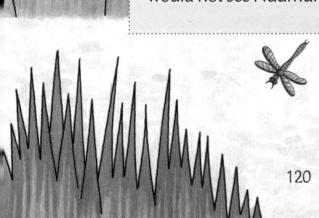
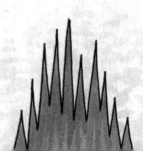

He just sent a rather strange message: "Wash seven times in the River Jordan. You will be healed."

Naaman wasn't sure he wanted to do that, but eventually he did as Elisha told him. He washed seven times in the river...and his skin was made completely better!

Naaman thanked Elisha and praised God for healing him.

Daniel in a strange land

Daniel 1

King Nebuchadnezzar of Babylon captured the king of Judah and stole treasures from the great Temple in Jerusalem. He also commanded that some of Israel's most handsome young men be brought back to Babylon. He brought Daniel and three friends, whom the king named Shadrach, Meshach, and Abednego. Nebuchadnezzar wanted them to study at the royal court for three years to

learn all about Babylon and study great books. Then they would serve the king.

The king wanted to give the young men food and drink, but they refused it because the king had offered it first to other gods. Instead they ate only vegetables and drank water.

Daniel and his friends were a long way from home. But they prayed to God and worked hard. They soon became the wisest and cleverest men in Babylon.

The king's dream

Daniel 2:1–47

King Nebuchadnezzar had a terrible nightmare. None of his wise men could explain the meaning of his dream. The king was very angry. He warned the wise men that he would kill them all if they couldn't help.

So Daniel asked God to show him the dream and its meaning.

The next day, he went to the king and explained what God had shown him. The king had seen a huge statue with a golden head, chest and arms of silver, a bronze body, iron legs, and clay feet. A stone from a mountain hit the feet, which crumbled, and the whole statue came crashing down.

"Your majesty," said Daniel. "You are indeed a great ruler, but after you will come three more kingdoms. Then God will set up a kingdom that will never fall."

The king bowed down low. "Now I believe that your God is above all other gods," he said.

The fiery furnace

Daniel 3

King Nebuchadnezzar ordered everyone
to bow down to his huge, golden statue.
But Daniel's friends — Shadrach, Meshach,
and Abednego — refused because this went
against God's command.

"Then throw them into the fiery furnace!"
said the king angrily.

"God will save us," said Shadrach,
Meshach, and Abednego.

The king ordered his men to heat the
furnace seven times hotter than usual.
Soldiers tied up Shadrach, Meshach,
and Abednego and threw them in.

The king watched.

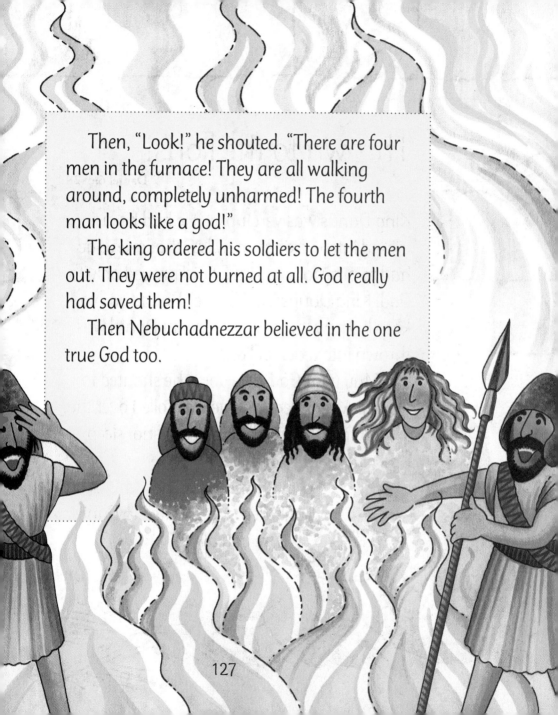

Then, "Look!" he shouted. "There are four men in the furnace! They are all walking around, completely unharmed! The fourth man looks like a god!"

The king ordered his soldiers to let the men out. They were not burned at all. God really had saved them!

Then Nebuchadnezzar believed in the one true God too.

Thrown to the lions!

Daniel 6:6–28

King Darius was very upset. He had been tricked into making a new law that everyone had to pray to him. But Daniel prayed only to God. King Darius liked Daniel. But he had to keep his new law and that meant Daniel was thrown into a den of lions.

"May your God save you!" he shouted to Daniel. A very heavy stone was rolled over the door of the den. The king could not sleep that night for worry.

Early the next day, he went to the lions' den and shouted to Daniel, "Are you alive?"

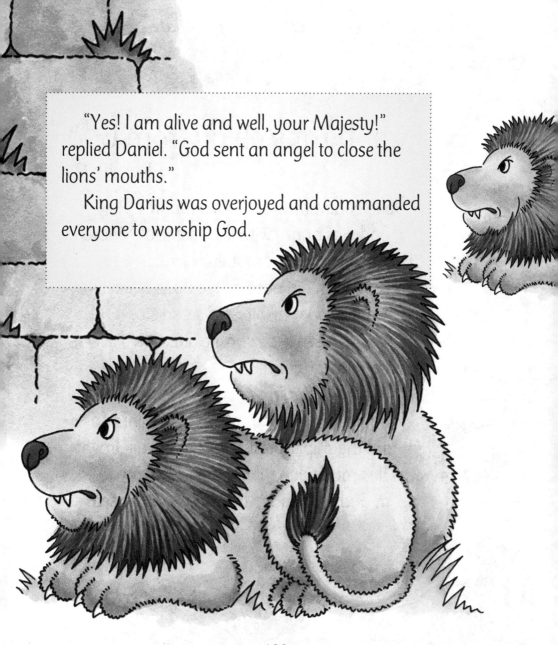

"Yes! I am alive and well, your Majesty!" replied Daniel. "God sent an angel to close the lions' mouths."

King Darius was overjoyed and commanded everyone to worship God.

129

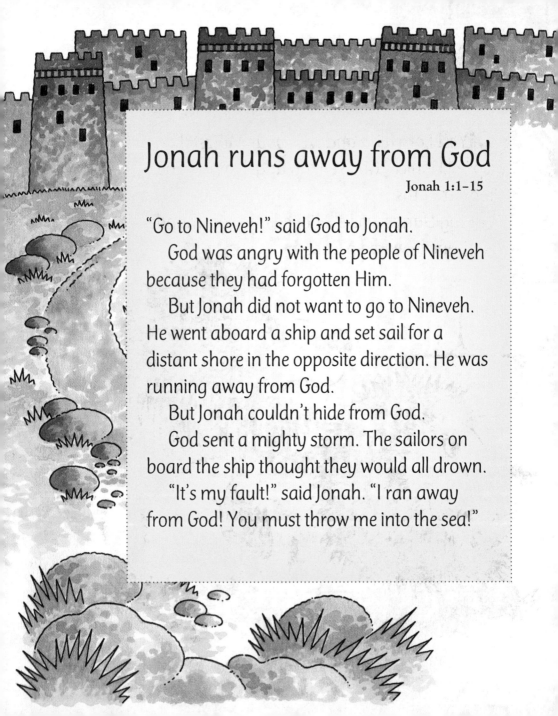

Jonah runs away from God

Jonah 1:1–15

"Go to Nineveh!" said God to Jonah.

God was angry with the people of Nineveh because they had forgotten Him.

But Jonah did not want to go to Nineveh. He went aboard a ship and set sail for a distant shore in the opposite direction. He was running away from God.

But Jonah couldn't hide from God.

God sent a mighty storm. The sailors on board the ship thought they would all drown.

"It's my fault!" said Jonah. "I ran away from God! You must throw me into the sea!"

At first the sailors didn't want to throw Jonah overboard. But the storm became worse and they were in great danger. So they threw Jonah out of the boat.

As soon as Jonah sank down into the dark water, the storm stopped.

131

Jonah and the big fish

Jonah 1:17; 2:10–3:5

But God saved Jonah from drowning.

He sent an enormous fish to come and swallow up Jonah. Inside the fish, Jonah prayed to God.

"Thank You for saving me!" he prayed. "You are a great God."

Jonah stayed inside the fish for three days and three nights. It was very dark and smelly. Then the fish spat him out onto a beach.

"Now go to Nineveh!" said God.

This time Jonah did as God said.

Jonah told the people of Nineveh that God wanted to show His love for them. He gave them a chance to say they were sorry for all the wrong things they had done and He forgave them.

The New Testament

Mary meets an angel

Luke 1:26–38, 46–55

God sent the angel Gabriel to a little town called Nazareth. He had come to give wonderful news to a virgin named Mary.

"Mary!" said Gabriel. "Don't be afraid! God has chosen you. You will have a baby boy and you must call Him Jesus. He will be very great. He will be the Son of God. His kingdom will never end!"

Mary was astonished and afraid, but she said to the angel, "I am God's servant. May it happen as you have said."

Mary sang songs of praise to God for choosing her to be the mother of God.

137

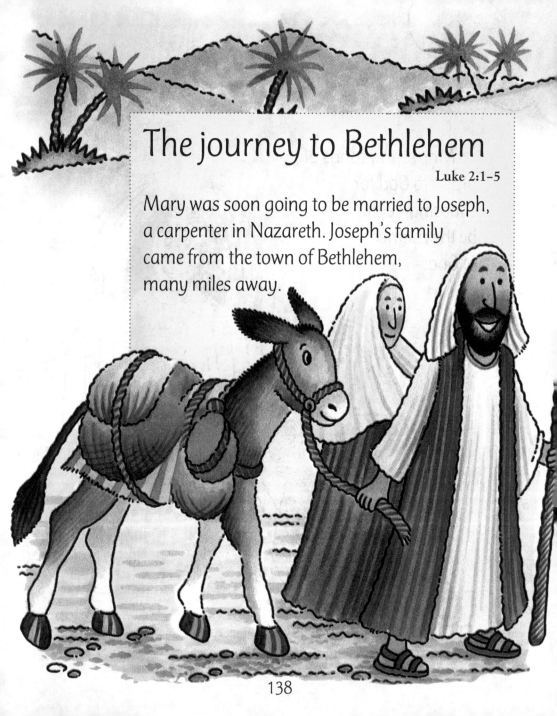

The journey to Bethlehem

Luke 2:1–5

Mary was soon going to be married to Joseph, a carpenter in Nazareth. Joseph's family came from the town of Bethlehem, many miles away.

Shortly before Mary's baby was due to be born, Joseph had to return to Bethlehem to be counted by the Roman governor. Mary had to go too.

It was a very long, tiring journey. Joseph walked in front, with Mary a little way behind. Their donkey carried their small bundles of clothes, and a water bottle.

Mary was getting very tired. Her baby was due to be born quite soon.

When would they reach Bethlehem?

No room at the inn

Luke 2:6–7

At last Mary and Joseph could see the rooftops of Bethlehem in the distance.

They were so tired after their long journey.

But when they arrived in Bethlehem, there was nowhere to stay!

Mary was very worried because her baby was soon to be born. Joseph knocked on many doors in the town, trying to find a room for them to sleep in that night.

At last an innkeeper said they could stay at the back of his house where the animals slept. There was no bed, but at least it was warm and dry in the straw.

Jesus is born

Luke 2:6–7

The time came for Mary to have her baby. She gave birth to a son.

Mary called Him Jesus, just as the angel Gabriel had told her to.

Mary wrapped the baby warmly in strips of cloth and laid Him in the soft hay in a manger.

The animals munched their food and shuffled in the straw. Mary gazed down at her little son. He looked so tiny and helpless. Yet the angel Gabriel had said that He was God, come to earth as a baby.

Angels visit the shepherds

Luke 2:8–14

On a hillside near Bethlehem some shepherds were looking after their sheep. Suddenly there was a blinding flash in the sky. It was an angel!

"Don't be afraid!" the angel said. "I have come to bring you good news. This very night a baby has been born in

Bethlehem. He is Christ the Lord!

"You will find the baby wrapped in strips of cloth and lying in a manger. Go now and see Him!"

The shepherds could not speak—they were very frightened and amazed at the same time. The Savior of the world had finally come!

Then lots of angels appeared in the sky, singing, "Glory to God in the highest, and on earth peace to men!"

The shepherds visit Jesus

Luke 2:15–20

"Hurry!" shouted the shepherds. "We must go to Bethlehem at once to find the baby God has told us about!"

They ran through the town, looking for a newborn baby.

"Is there a baby here?" they asked an innkeeper.

He showed the shepherds through to the back of the house, where the animals slept. There they found Mary and Joseph. And there, in a manger, wrapped in cloths, was the newborn baby: Jesus, their Savior.

The shepherds looked at the tiny baby and felt great joy in their hearts.

They went back to their sheep, praising God for all they had seen. It was just as the angel had said.

Wise Men see a new star

Matthew 2:1–2

When Jesus was born in Bethlehem, Wise Men in lands far away in the east spotted a very bright star in the sky. They knew it was a sign.

"A new king is born!" said one Wise Man.

"Let's go and find Him!" said another.

They chose special gifts to take with them, set off, and followed the star.

They traveled over desert, hills, and valleys to find the new King.

149

Following the star Matthew 2:1–8

The Wise Men went to the palace of King Herod.

"Do you know where the new King has been born?" they asked Herod.

King Herod was jealous. He wanted to be the only king.

He asked the chief priests and teachers to find out what the Wise Men were talking about.

"It is written in the Scriptures," said one teacher, "that a king will be born in Bethlehem!"

Herod started to make plans.

"Go and find the baby in Bethlehem!" he told the Wise Men. "But please come back and tell me where He is so I can worship Him too."

Jesus at the Temple

Luke 2:22–32

When Jesus was just over a month old, Mary and Joseph took Him to the Temple in Jerusalem. They wanted to say thank You to God.

They took two doves to offer at the Temple.

In the Temple there was a very old man named Simeon who had been waiting all his life to see the Savior. Simeon saw Mary and knew at once that her baby was the special Child

he had been waiting to see. He took Jesus in his arms and thanked God:

"Lord God, now I may go in peace, for I have seen the Savior, the one who will bring light to all the people of God."

Gifts for the baby king

Matthew 2:9–15

The Wise Men followed the star all the way to Bethlehem, where they found Jesus with His mother, Mary. They were overjoyed to see Him. They bowed down low and worshiped Jesus. Then out of their saddlebags they pulled their fine gifts and gave them to Jesus: gold, frankincense, and myrrh.

God warned the Wise Men in a dream not to go back to King Herod, so they went home by a different road. And God warned Joseph to take Mary and Jesus to Egypt, where they would be safe from wicked King Herod.

Jesus goes missing

Luke 2:41–49

When Jesus was twelve years old, He went to the city of Jerusalem for the Passover feast.

When it was time to go home, Mary and Joseph couldn't see Jesus, but they thought He

was traveling with others. Then Mary began to get very worried and turned back to Jerusalem to look for Jesus.

Three days later, Mary and Joseph found Him. He was in the Temple courts, speaking to the teachers. Everyone was amazed. Jesus knew so much about God!

"My son!" said Mary. "We've been so worried!"

"Mother," said Jesus. "Didn't you know I would be here in My Father's house?"

Jesus is baptized

Luke 3:2-3, 21-22

John the Baptist talked to people about God. He told them to say sorry for the wrong things they had done. Then John baptized them in the water of the River Jordan for the forgiveness of their sins.

When Jesus was about thirty years old, He came to see John on the bank of the river.

"I want you to baptize Me in the river," said Jesus.

John was very surprised. Jesus had done nothing wrong and John thought He didn't need to be baptized. But he did as Jesus asked.

When Jesus came out of the river, the Holy Spirit came upon Him in the form of a dove, and a voice from heaven spoke: "This is My Son, with whom I am pleased."

It was God's voice.

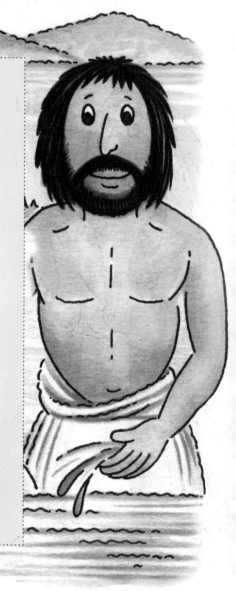

Jesus in the wilderness

Matthew 4

After Jesus was baptized, He went into the wilderness and ate nothing for forty days and nights. When He was very hungry, the devil came and tempted Him.

First, the devil tried to persuade Jesus to turn stones into bread to eat. Next, Jesus was taken to the top of the Temple and told to throw

Himself off so the angels would catch Him. Last, the devil offered to give Jesus all the kingdoms of the earth if He would only bow down and worship him. But Jesus did not give in to any of the devil's tricks.

"Away from Me!" Jesus said.

He spoke words from the Scriptures to the devil until he went away and left Jesus alone. Then angels came to be with Jesus.

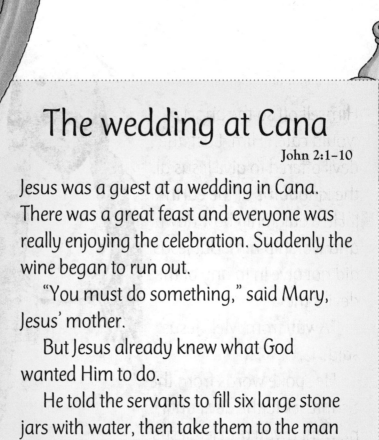

The wedding at Cana

John 2:1–10

Jesus was a guest at a wedding in Cana. There was a great feast and everyone was really enjoying the celebration. Suddenly the wine began to run out.

"You must do something," said Mary, Jesus' mother.

But Jesus already knew what God wanted Him to do.

He told the servants to fill six large stone jars with water, then take them to the man in charge of the feast. When the man tasted it, he was very pleased.

"That's strange!" said the man. "People usually serve the best wine first, but you have left the best wine till last!"

Jesus had actually turned water into wine!

Jesus calls the disciples

Luke 5:1–11

One day Jesus was speaking to large crowds of people on the shore of Lake Galilee. He was telling them about God's kingdom.

Jesus saw two fishermen's boats on the shore. He stepped into a boat belonging to Simon and spoke to the crowds from the boat.

When He had finished speaking, Jesus asked Simon to row the boat out into the deeper water and let down the nets.

"We've worked hard all night," said Simon, "and haven't caught a single fish. But if You tell me, I'll do it."

So off they went. They let down their nets and when they pulled them

back up, they were filled to overflowing with fish!

Simon couldn't believe his eyes. Neither could James and John, Simon's partners.

"Don't be afraid," said Jesus. "Follow Me. I will make you fishers of men."

The fishermen left their nets and followed Jesus.

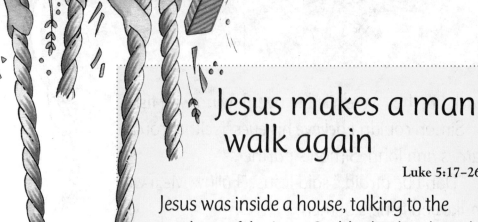

Jesus makes a man walk again

Luke 5:17–26

Jesus was inside a house, talking to the teachers of the Law. Suddenly, they heard a rustling noise above them and saw a large hole appear in the ceiling!

Faces peered through the hole, and a man on a mat was lowered down through the hole. The man could not walk and he wanted to see Jesus very badly. His friends could not bring him through the door because of the huge crowds, so they had taken him to the roof and thought of another way in— through the ceiling!

Jesus looked at the man kindly.

"Your sins are forgiven," He said. "Stand up! Pick up your mat and walk."

At once the man stood up and walked home on his strong legs, thanking God for what Jesus had done.

Jesus and the tax collector

Luke 5:27–32

Matthew was a tax collector. Everyone hated tax collectors, so Matthew was often unhappy and alone.

Jesus stopped to talk to Matthew as he was sitting at his usual place to collect the taxes.

"Come and follow Me!" He said kindly.

Matthew stood up and went away with Jesus.

Matthew held a big feast that day for Jesus at his home. He invited other tax collectors and friends.

Some teachers of the Law complained. "Why do You eat and drink with those people?" they asked.

Jesus heard what they were saying and answered, "It is not healthy people who need a doctor, but those who are ill. Go and think about what that means."

Jesus wanted everyone to know that they could come to God and be forgiven.

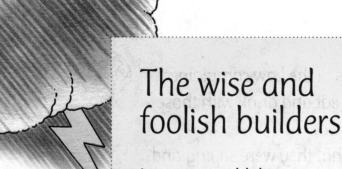

The wise and foolish builders

Luke 6:46–49

Jesus once told this story:

"Anyone who listens to My words and does what I say is like a wise man who built his house upon a rock," said Jesus.

"The rain poured down, the wind blew hard, the rivers rose and tried to wash the house away. But the man had built his house on a strong foundation. It didn't budge.

"But if you don't listen to what I say, you are like a foolish man who built his house upon the sand.

"The rain poured down, the wind blew

hard, the rivers rose and tried to wash the house away. And the house fell down with an enormous CRASH!"

The soldier's servant

Matthew 8:5–13

Crowds followed Jesus everywhere, watching to see what He would do for people who were sick or blind. He did amazing things!

One day, a Roman officer came to Jesus for help.

"My servant is very ill," he said. "He is too ill to leave the house."

Jesus replied, "Then I will go to your house and make him well."

"No, no," said the officer. "I know how busy You are. But if

You just say the word, I know he will be healed."

Jesus was very pleased to find that the officer had great faith in Him.

"Go home, then," said Jesus. "What you believe will be done."

The officer ran home. He found to his great joy that his servant had been made well again!

The sower

Luke 8:4–15

Jesus told this story
to a large crowd on
the shores of Lake
Galilee:

"A man went
to sow some corn.
Some seed fell along
the path where birds
came and ate it.
Some seed fell
on rocky ground
where the corn
could not grow.

174

"Some seed fell among thorn bushes that choked the plants.

"But some of the seeds fell in good soil. The plants grew and produced fine corn and there was a good harvest."

Jesus explained what the story meant:

God is the sower. The seed is His message. Some people hear God's message but forget about Him. Some people try to follow God but give up when trouble comes their way.

Some people become too busy with worries, money, and all kinds of other things.

But other people are like good soil where the seeds can grow and blossom; they hear God's message, follow God, and live for Him.

The hidden treasure

Matthew 13:44

Jesus told another story about what the kingdom of God is like:

"A man found some treasure hidden in a field. It was so beautiful! It sparkled in the sunlight and the man wanted to keep it.

"So the man went away and sold everything that he had in the world, even his clothes! With the money he got, he bought the field with the treasure in it. Now the treasure belonged to him! He was really happy!"

Jesus calms the storm

Mark 4:35–41

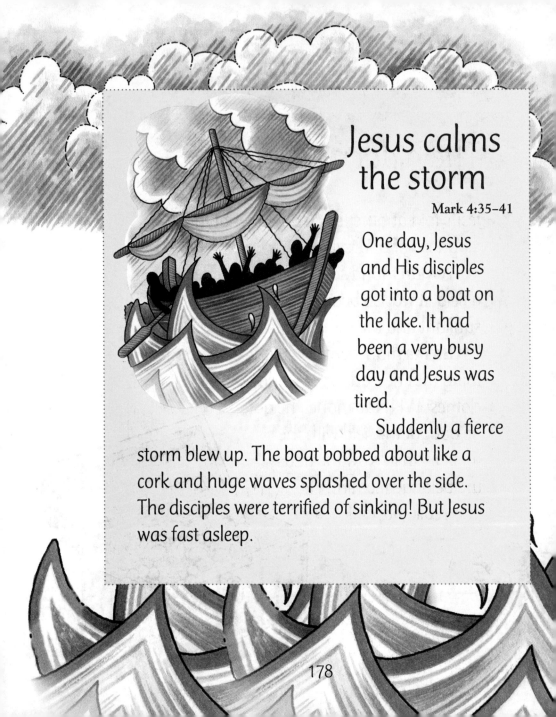

One day, Jesus and His disciples got into a boat on the lake. It had been a very busy day and Jesus was tired.

Suddenly a fierce storm blew up. The boat bobbed about like a cork and huge waves splashed over the side. The disciples were terrified of sinking! But Jesus was fast asleep.

"Save us, Lord!" they shouted to Jesus.

"Why are you so afraid?" asked Jesus, waking up.

Then Jesus got up and ordered the wind and the waves to calm down. The storm vanished. Everyone was amazed.

"Even the winds and the waves obey Him!" they said.

Jesus brings Jairus's daughter back to life

Mark 5:21–42

One day, hundreds of people were crowding around Jesus.

"Please help me!" begged a man called Jairus. "My daughter is very ill."

As Jesus tried to make His way to Jairus's house, people kept stopping Him.

Then someone from Jairus's house came to Jesus.

"It's too late now," he said. "Jairus's daughter has died!"

"Don't worry," said Jesus to Jairus. "Just believe, and she will be well."

Jesus went to the house with Jairus and three of Jesus' disciples. Everyone was crying loudly and sobbing.

But Jesus said, "Don't worry! She is not dead. She is only asleep."

He took the girl by the hand and said, "Get up!"

She came back to life and sat up.

"Give her something to eat," said Jesus.

Jairus and the girl's mother were overjoyed to see their daughter alive again.

Jesus feeds five thousand people

John 6:1–13

Jesus was speaking to a large crowd of men, women, and children. They had been listening to Him all day and were getting hungry.

Jesus wanted to feed them.

"Where can we buy food for all these people?" He asked His disciples.

Philip replied, "We would need more than two hundred silver coins to buy enough!"

Andrew said, "There is a boy here who says he will share his lunch. But he has only five loaves and two small fishes."

Jesus took the food, thanked God, then shared it with everyone!

No one went away hungry. Jesus gave them all enough to eat, and there were even twelve baskets full of leftovers!

The good Samaritan

Luke 10:25–37

A man once asked Jesus, "Who is my neighbor?"
Jesus told the man this story:

"One day, a man was attacked and left for
dead while travelling from Jerusalem to Jericho.

"After some time, a priest travelling that
way saw the injured man lying by the roadside.
But he walked on by.

"Next a temple-worker walked past. He
didn't stop either!

"Finally a man from Samaria came along the
road. He bandaged the wounds of the injured
man, helped him onto his donkey, and took him
to an inn, paying the innkeeper to look after
him until he was better."

Jesus asked, "Who was the poor man's real neighbor?"

"The one who helped him," replied the man.

The man with the barns

Luke 12:16–21

Jesus told this story:

"There was once a young man who was very rich. He stored his crops in a barn. When the barn became too full, he thought he would just build bigger barns. Then he said to himself, "Now I've stored up good things for many years. I'll eat, drink, and take life easy.

"But God spoke to him: 'You fool! Tonight your life will be taken from you. Who will get all your riches then?'"

Jesus said, "This is how it will be for people who are greedy and keep things for themselves but do not give much to God."

Jesus walks on the water

Matthew 14:22–33

Jesus' disciples set off in a boat to cross the lake and go to Capernaum. A stormy wind blew and waves rocked the boat. The men kept on rowing, but they were scared.

Suddenly they saw someone coming toward them. He was walking on the water! They couldn't believe what they saw and were very afraid.

"Don't be frightened," said Jesus. "You all know Me—your Lord, Jesus."

Only Jesus could walk on water!

They wanted Him to come aboard. At once the boat reached the shore and they were all safe.

The lost sheep

Luke 15:1–7

Jesus once told a story about a shepherd:

"A shepherd had a hundred sheep. He looked after them all and protected them from wild animals.

"One day the shepherd found that one was missing. So he set out to find his lost sheep, leaving the ninety-nine other sheep in the sheepfold.

"He looked high and low, behind bushes and rocks. Where could the sheep be?

"Suddenly the shepherd heard faint bleating: he had found his lost sheep!

"He picked it up lovingly and carried it home on his shoulders.

"He was so pleased to have found his lost sheep that he invited all his neighbors to a party.

"God is like that shepherd," said Jesus. "He cares even if only one of His sheep is lost."

The prodigal son

Luke 15:11–24

Jesus once told a story about a son who left home with his share of his inheritance:

"The father loved his son and was very sad.

"The son did many things and spent all the money very quickly. But then nobody wanted to be his friend anymore. He had to find a job feeding pigs and he was hungry.

"'I must go to Dad and ask to work on the farm,' he thought.

"As he came near to his home, he saw his father running toward him. The son he loved had come back. How happy that made him!

"That father was like God," Jesus explained. "He waits to forgive anyone who comes back to Him to say they are sorry."

The rich young man

Luke 18:18–30

A rich young ruler asked Jesus, "What must I do to live with God forever?"

"Do what God tells you in the Ten Commandments," said Jesus.

"I've kept them all my life," said the young man.

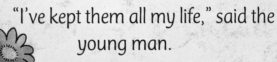

"Then sell everything you have and give it all to the poor," said Jesus. "Come, follow Me."

The young man was very sad because he was very rich and didn't want to give away all his wealth.

Jesus said, "It is hard for rich people to enter God's kingdom. It is easier for a camel to go through the eye of a needle!"

The man with leprosy

Matthew 8:1–4

Jesus went with His disciples to a nearby town. They met a man there who had a terrible skin disease called leprosy. His skin had turned all white. Nobody went near the man. He was very lonely.

When the man saw Jesus coming, he threw himself at Jesus' feet, crying, "Lord, You can make me well again, if You want to."

Jesus put His hand on the man and said, "Yes, I do want to make you well. Be well again!" All at once, the man's skin turned a normal color and he was completely well again!

Jesus told him not to tell anyone about it, but to go to the priest:

"Show him that you are well again and offer a gift to God. Everyone will know that God has healed you."

News about Jesus spread throughout the town.

Jesus blesses children

Luke 18:15–17

People loved to bring their children to Jesus for Him to bless them.

Jesus welcomed them with open arms.

But Jesus' disciples thought He had more important things to do than talk to children.

"Don't bother Him with the children," they said to the mothers and fathers.

Jesus overheard them and became angry.

"Let the children come to Me!" He said. "Don't try to stop them!

"My kingdom belongs to people who are like these children. You will never enter God's kingdom if you don't enter it like a child."

Jesus makes a blind man see

Mark 8:22–25

One day people brought a blind man to Jesus. They wanted Jesus to help him to see again.

Jesus walked out of the village with the man. Then Jesus spat on the man's eyes and gently put His hands on them.

"Can you see anything yet?" asked Jesus.

"I can see some people, but they are all fuzzy, like trees walking around."

So Jesus put His hands on the man's eyes a second time. This time the man opened his eyes and could see perfectly!
He was amazed to see the colorful world and the kind face of Jesus.

Zacchaeus

Luke 19:1–10

Jesus was walking through Jericho. A man named Zacchaeus lived there. He was a very rich man and was in charge of collecting taxes in the area.

Zacchaeus was a very short man. He heard that Jesus was coming, but he wasn't tall enough to see over the heads of the crowd. So he climbed a tree to see Jesus.

Jesus called to him in the tree: "Zacchaeus, come down! I want to come to your house today."

Zacchaeus was very pleased to welcome Jesus to his house. But other people started complaining, "Zacchaeus is a bad man! Why does Jesus want to eat with him?"

Zacchaeus later told the crowds of people that he was going to be nicer to everyone.

"I want to give half of all I own to the poor. If I have cheated anyone, I will pay them back four times as much."

The wise and foolish girls

Matthew 25:1–13

Jesus told a story about ten girls at a wedding:

"There were once ten girls who were supposed to meet the bridegroom on his way to the wedding. They carried oil lamps to light the way. But the oil didn't last long in the lamps.

"Five of the girls remembered to bring extra oil with them. But the other five had

forgotten. Their lamps went out and they
had to run off to buy more.

"While they were away, the bridegroom
arrived. The five girls whose lamps were
burning brightly met him and went with him
to the wedding. The door was shut.

"When the other five girls finally arrived,
they were too late for the wedding!"

Jesus said we should be like the wise girls
and be ready for Him when He comes again.

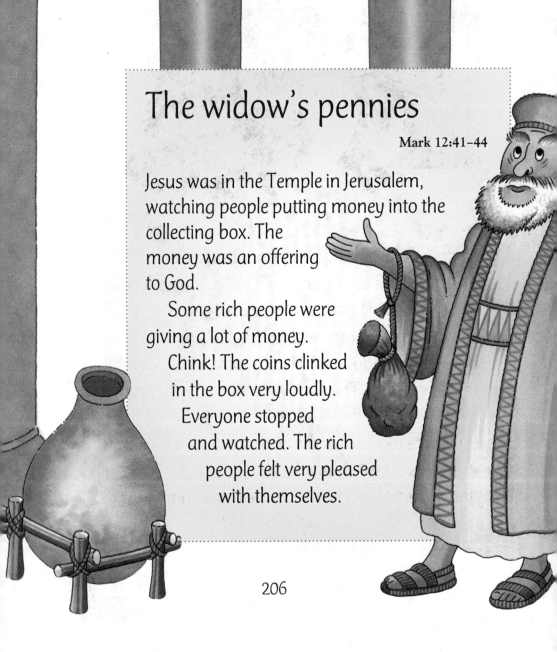

The widow's pennies

Mark 12:41-44

Jesus was in the Temple in Jerusalem, watching people putting money into the collecting box. The money was an offering to God.

Some rich people were giving a lot of money.

Chink! The coins clinked in the box very loudly. Everyone stopped and watched. The rich people felt very pleased with themselves.

Then a very poor widow shuffled toward the collecting box. She didn't want anyone to notice her. She was ashamed that she had only two very small coins to give to God.

Clink! The two small coins dropped softly into the box.

The widow moved quietly away. Jesus told His disciples to come closer to Him.

"Let Me tell you," He said, "that poor widow has just given more than anyone else.

"Everyone else gave what they didn't really need. But this widow gave everything she has to God."

207

Lazarus

John 11:1–44

Jesus had a good friend named Lazarus, who lived in a town many miles away. Jesus heard that Lazarus was ill. But by the time Jesus reached the town, Lazarus was dead.

Jesus wept. He went to the tomb where Lazarus's body was put. It had been there for four days already. A large stone was rolled across the tomb.

Jesus told some men to roll the stone aside. He prayed aloud to God: "Thank You, Father, that You hear My prayers."

Then Jesus shouted, "Come out, Lazarus!"
Lazarus walked out into the daylight,
still covered in his grave clothes and with
a cloth over his face, but he was alive again!

Many people watching now knew that
Jesus had been sent from God and
they put their trust in Him.

A welcome for the King

Matthew 21:1–9

Jesus and His disciples were going to Jerusalem for the Passover festival.

Jesus sent two of His followers ahead, saying, "Go to the village over there and find a young donkey. Bring it to Me. Say that your master needs it."

The two friends fetched the donkey and put their cloaks over the donkey's back.

Jesus rode into the great city of Jerusalem. Huge crowds came to greet Jesus, spreading their cloaks on the road and waving palm branches.

"Hosanna to the Son of David! Blessed is He who comes in the name of the Lord!" they shouted.

They cheered and waved to Jesus, their King.

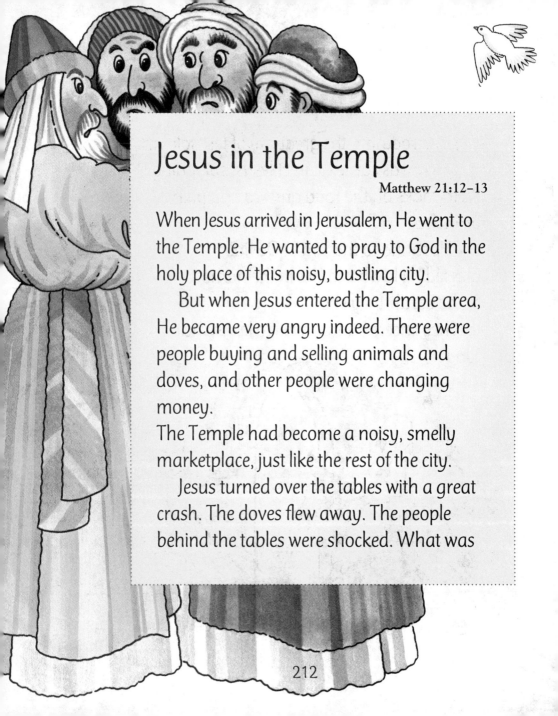

Jesus in the Temple

Matthew 21:12–13

When Jesus arrived in Jerusalem, He went to the Temple. He wanted to pray to God in the holy place of this noisy, bustling city.

But when Jesus entered the Temple area, He became very angry indeed. There were people buying and selling animals and doves, and other people were changing money.
The Temple had become a noisy, smelly marketplace, just like the rest of the city.

Jesus turned over the tables with a great crash. The doves flew away. The people behind the tables were shocked. What was

Jesus doing?

"You are turning the Temple into a place for robbers!" shouted Jesus. "It is written, 'My house shall be called a house of prayer!'"

Jesus wanted to keep the Temple a holy place. But what He did made many people angry. The chief priests and teachers of the Law began to make plans to get rid of Jesus.

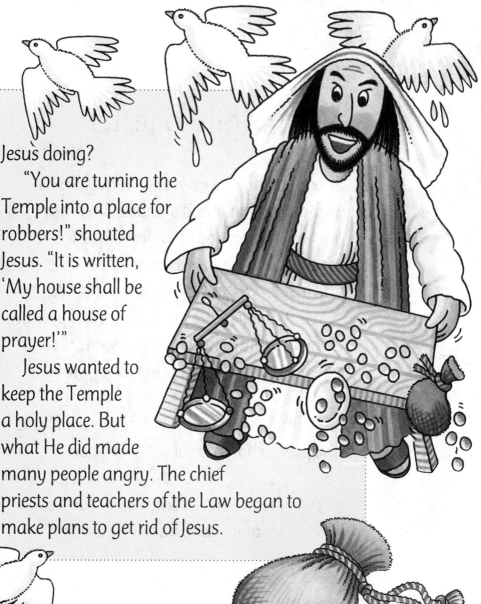

213

Mary's gift to Jesus

Mark 14:3–9

Shortly before the Passover festival, Jesus went to eat at a friend's house. A woman named Mary came up to Jesus holding a very precious jar. It was made of alabaster and inside was something very special.

Mary opened the jar. The smell of perfume came out. Mary had brought some very expensive perfume for Jesus. She poured it over His head.

"What's she doing?" asked some of Jesus' disciples. "That's a real waste of money, just pouring it away like that!"

Jesus heard them complaining and said, "Leave her alone. She has done a beautiful thing for Me to prepare My body for burial."

Judas betrays Jesus

Matthew 26:14–16

The chief priests wanted to get rid of Jesus. But they didn't know how to capture Him.

Judas Iscariot, one of Jesus' disciples, was very greedy for money. He thought of a plan to get rich quickly.

Judas went to the chief priests and asked, "What will you pay me if I hand Jesus over to you?"

"We'll give you thirty pieces of silver," they said.

"I'll do it!" said Judas.

Judas watched for a chance to hand Jesus over to them. He was no longer a friend of Jesus. Judas was His enemy.

217

Jesus washes His disciples' feet John 13:4–14

Jesus knew He would not be with His disciples for much longer. He wanted to celebrate the Passover meal with them one last time.

Jesus met His twelve disciples at the upper room of a house in Jerusalem.

Jesus took a bowl of water and began to wash His disciples' feet.

"You mustn't wash my feet!" said Peter. "You are our Master, not our servant!"

"Unless I do, you don't belong to Me," said Jesus.

"Then wash my hands and head as well!" said Peter.

Jesus washed Peter's feet.

"Now that I have washed your feet," said Jesus, "you must also wash each other's feet. Do as I have done."

219

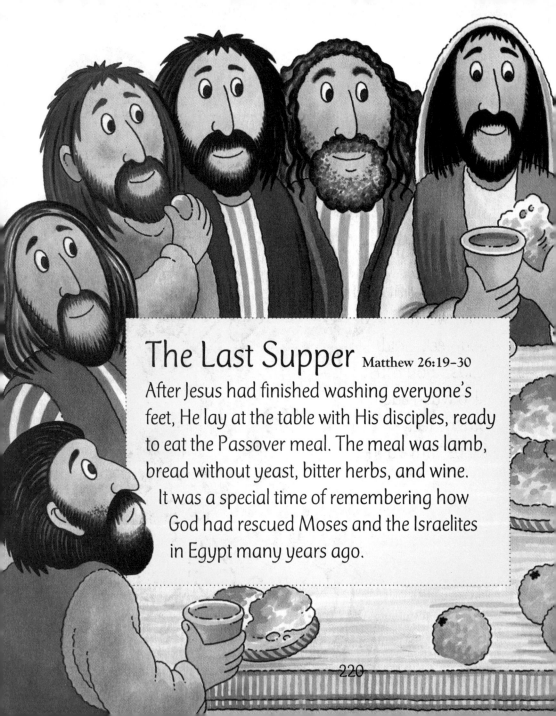

The Last Supper Matthew 26:19–30

After Jesus had finished washing everyone's feet, He lay at the table with His disciples, ready to eat the Passover meal. The meal was lamb, bread without yeast, bitter herbs, and wine. It was a special time of remembering how God had rescued Moses and the Israelites in Egypt many years ago.

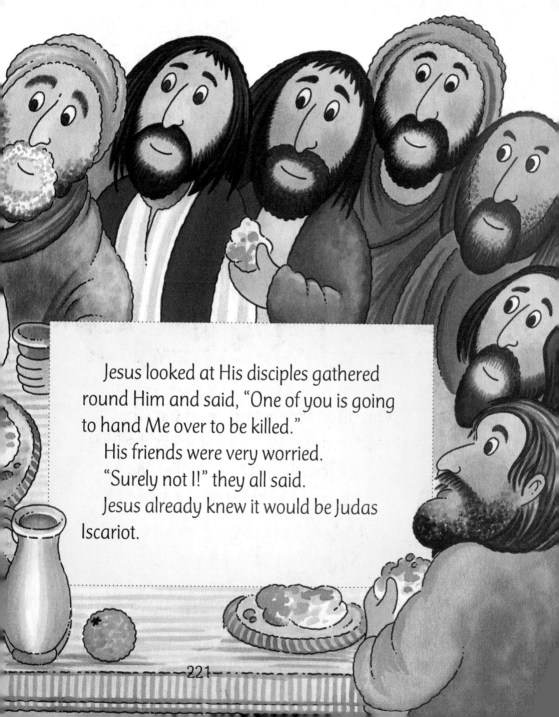

Jesus looked at His disciples gathered round Him and said, "One of you is going to hand Me over to be killed."

His friends were very worried.

"Surely not I!" they all said.

Jesus already knew it would be Judas Iscariot.

While they were eating, Jesus took the
bread, broke it, and gave it to His disciples.
"Eat this and remember Me,"
said Jesus.

222

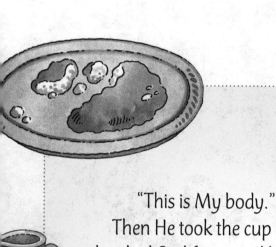

"This is My body."

Then He took the cup of wine, thanked God for it, and handed it round.

"Drink this and remember Me," said Jesus. "This is My blood, given for you for the forgiveness of sins."

Jesus' disciples drank the wine. They sang a song together, then went away to the Mount of Olives.

223

Gethsemane

Matthew 26:36–41

On the Mount of Olives was a garden called Gethsemane. Here Jesus knelt down to pray to God. He knew that the time was coming for Him to be taken away. He was very sad. Tears ran down His face as He prayed to God, His Father.

Jesus asked His disciples to pray with Him. But they kept falling asleep.

"Why are you sleeping?" He asked them. "Watch and pray with Me."

Jesus is arrested

Matthew 26:47–57

Suddenly a crowd came toward them and Judas Iscariot was with them. Soldiers and chief priests followed closely behind. Judas came near to Jesus to kiss Him. This showed the soldiers where Jesus was.

One of Jesus' disciples took out a sword and chopped off the ear of

the high priest's servant!

"Put that sword away!" said Jesus. "All who use the sword will die by the sword. Things must happen in this way."

Jesus touched the servant's ear and healed it.

Jesus was arrested and taken away to see the high priest.

Peter pretends he doesn't know Jesus

Matthew 26:69–75

Jesus' other disciples were very upset, especially Peter. Earlier that evening, Jesus had warned Peter:

"Before the rooster crows tonight, you will say three times that you do not know Me."

Peter couldn't understand it. Jesus was his friend! Peter wouldn't let Him down.

But while Peter was waiting to see what would happen to Jesus, some girls came up to him and asked if he was a friend of Jesus.

"No," said Peter. "I don't know what you are talking about!"

They asked him three times and each time he said, "No!"

Then suddenly a rooster crowed. Peter remembered what Jesus had said.

Peter felt terrible and cried. He had wanted to be faithful to Jesus, but now he really had let Jesus down.

Jesus is taken to Pilate

Mark 15:1–20

The soldiers who were guarding Jesus were very cruel to Him. Then Jesus was brought before Pilate, the Roman governor. "What has this man done wrong?" Pilate asked the crowd.

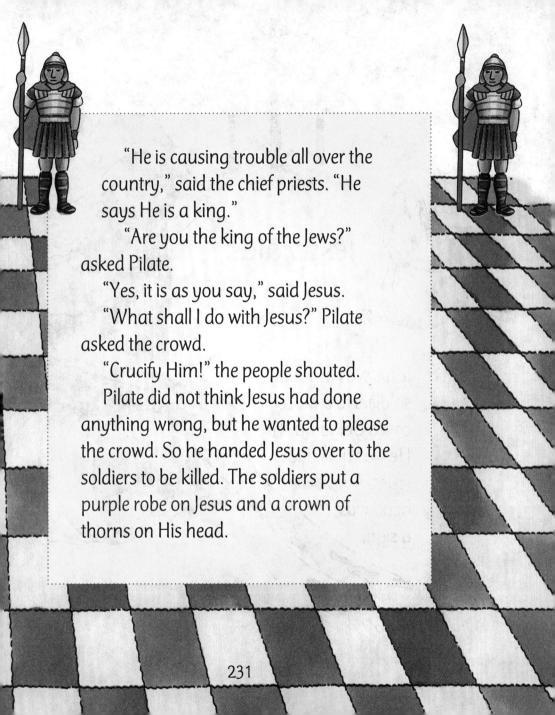

"He is causing trouble all over the country," said the chief priests. "He says He is a king."

"Are you the king of the Jews?" asked Pilate.

"Yes, it is as you say," said Jesus.

"What shall I do with Jesus?" Pilate asked the crowd.

"Crucify Him!" the people shouted.

Pilate did not think Jesus had done anything wrong, but he wanted to please the crowd. So he handed Jesus over to the soldiers to be killed. The soldiers put a purple robe on Jesus and a crown of thorns on His head.

Jesus dies on a cross

Mark 15:22–37

Jesus was taken by the soldiers to a place called Golgotha. There He was nailed to a cross. Above His head was a sign,

"The King of the Jews."
Jesus' mother, Mary,
stood close by and
watched. How could
they do this to her
precious son?

Darkness covered
the land. At the ninth
hour, Jesus cried out in
a loud voice to God, then
breathed His last breath.
Jesus died.

A Roman soldier near
the cross saw this. He said,
"Truly, this man was
the Son of God."

The women find
the tomb empty

Luke 24:1–3

Early on Sunday morning, the third day after Jesus died, some of the women went to His tomb with special spices.

But what a shock they had when they got there! The large stone that blocked the entrance to the tomb had been rolled away! When they looked inside, they did not see Jesus' body.

The tomb was empty!

"Jesus is alive!" Luke 24:4–8

Jesus' body was gone. All that was left were the strips of cloth Jesus' body had been wrapped in.

Suddenly two men in bright shining clothes appeared.

"Don't look for Jesus here," they said. "He is alive! Remember that He told you He would die and rise again

on the third day."
The women suddenly
remembered.
They ran home
at once and told
Jesus' apostles.
Very soon
they all saw
Jesus again for
them-selves.
It was true! Jesus
really was alive!

The amazing catch of fish

John 21:1–6

Over the next few days, Jesus appeared to His disciples and many others and showed them He really was alive again.

Peter and a group of disciples were out fishing in their boat. Early the next morning, Jesus came to see them and stood on the shore. He was far away, so they did not recognize Him.

"Haven't you caught any fish?" He shouted to the fishermen.

"No!" said Peter.

"Then throw your net on the other side of the boat," said Jesus, "and you will catch plenty!"

The men did as He said and sure enough, their nets were filled to the bursting point with fresh, wriggling fish.

239

Breakfast on the beach

John 21:7–14

"It's Jesus!" said Peter.

Peter and the other apostles knew that only God could do something so amazing. They knew Jesus was the Lord.

Jesus had made a small fire on the shore to cook some of the fish. He had some bread for them too. His disciples came and sat with Him and ate breakfast on the beach. It was wonderful to be with the Lord Jesus again!

241

Jesus returns to heaven

Acts 1:4–11

Jesus saw His apostles many times over the next few days and preached about the kingdom of God.

"Don't leave Jerusalem," He told His apostles, "but wait for the gift God has promised—to baptize you with the Holy Spirit. When He comes, you will be able to tell the whole world about Me!"

After forty days, Jesus was taken up to heaven. He was hidden from sight by a cloud.

As the disciples were looking at the sky, two men in white clothes stood beside them.

"Why are you looking at the sky?" they asked the disciples. "Jesus will return one day in the same way as you saw Him go."

The Holy Spirit comes to the believers

Acts 2:1–6

A few days later, on the day of Pentecost, all of Jesus' apostles met together in one place.

Suddenly there was a noise from heaven that sounded like a strong wind blowing. The noise filled the whole house. Then tongues that looked like fire appeared on each one. Everyone was filled with the Holy Spirit and could suddenly speak all kinds of different languages!

There were people in Jerusalem from many different countries, but they could all understand Jesus' apostles speak of the mighty works of God in their own language.

Peter speaks about Jesus

Acts 2:22–42

Peter stood up and told the crowds about Jesus—how He had come to show God's power and be put to death on a cross to pay for their sins. Peter told how God had made Jesus come

alive again to defeat death. And he explained that Jesus kept the promises of the Old Testament.

"Repent and be baptized in the name of Christ for the forgiveness of sin, and you will be given the Holy Spirit," said Peter.

That day, three thousand people were baptized into the kingdom of God!

Jesus' disciples were often in danger. But God helped them not to be afraid. They wanted people all over the world to know the good news that God loves the world so much that He sent His Son, Jesus, to save His people from their sins by dying on the cross.

Where to find the stories in the Bible

This edition published in 2009 by Concordia Publishing House

First edition 2005

Copyright © 2005 AD Publishing Services Ltd
1 Churchgates, The Wilderness, Berkhamsted, Herts HP4 2UB
Bible stories copyright © 2005 AD Publishing Services Ltd, Leena Lane
Illustrations copyright © 2005 Gillian Chapman

Manufactured in the United States of America, 036670, 092160.

Editorial director: Annette Reynolds
Art director: Gerald Rogers
Pre-production: Krystyna Hewitt
Production: John Laister

2   3   4   5   6   7   8   9   10   17 16 15 14 13 12 11 10 09

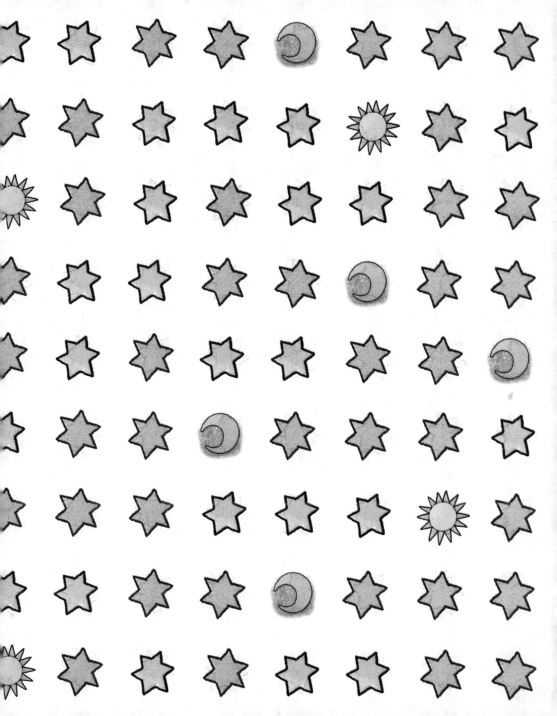